Down By The Riverside

BY RONNIE MCBRAYER

ALSO BY RONNIE MCBRAYER

But God Meant It for Good

Keeping the Faith: Passages, Proverbs, and Parables

Leaving Religion, Following Jesus

Keeping the Faith, Volume 2

The Jesus Tribe

Esther

How Far Is Heaven?

The Gospel According to Waffle House

Fruits of the Cotton Patch

Wild Wild Walton

May the Road Rise to Meet You

Down By The Riverside

Ronnie McBrayer

ACKNOWLEDGEMENT

The stories contained within this book are historically based in the folklore tradition. As such, elements of fact, oral storytelling, and narration are combined to create a genre unique to itself. This work was inspired and largely based on the 2016 Grit & Grace production, "Down By The Riverside." Where applicable, those stories are used by Grit & Grace's express permission.

Grit & Grace is the Official Folk Life Production of Walton County; a non-profit community based theater group whose mission and purpose is to preserve the history of Walton County, Florida through storytelling, music, and dance based on the stories and legends of Walton County.

Post Office Box 62, DeFuniak Springs, Florida 32435 www.gritandgrace.org

i

CONTENTS

INTRODUCTION

"When a wise man points at the moon," goes the Chinese proverb often attributed to Confucius, "the fool only examines the finger." Such "foolishness" is a common trap, and we fall into it easily, distracted by the messenger or medium – what is only the pointer – and miss the light of the message itself.

This little book, like its partner play and script, "Down By The Riverside," presented by Grit & Grace in the summer of 2016, is only a tool. An implement. A device. A pointer. To what do these point? To the light of our personal and communal histories; to the radiance of the heroes who have lived before us and continue to abide with us; to the illuminated past, where our roots dig into the sandy soil of the Florida Panhandle, sustain us, and move us on toward the future. Thus, books such as this one – along with any accompanying scripts, songs, or theatrical performances – are like road signs. They show us where we have been, and show us where we are headed.

It's not unlike the millions of vacationers who visit our coastal beaches every year. They make plans, save money, and count the days until they can be on their way. Driving from Atlanta, Nashville, Birmingham, Houston, and points beyond, eventually they begin to encounter signs with directional arrows that say, "Beaches" or "Grayton" or "Santa Rosa Beach." How foolish would it be if these travelers stopped at one of these signs and unloaded their SUVs along the side of the road? What if beach chairs, coolers, and bicycles spilled out on the ground; as mothers slather children with sunblock; and calls are made back home to tell the family that they had safely arrived at their destination?

Of course, such travelers haven't arrived anywhere. They have only stopped to marvel at a signpost, something never intended to be an end unto itself. The sign is there only to point these adventurers toward a much more majestic, more satisfying destination. Let this book be received the same way. Let it serve as an arrow pointing you to the real destination: Our rich, local history and the magnificent people who wrote and lived it.

The people in this book, as the title implies, are people of the river, specifically the Choctawhatchee River. The Choctawhatchee forms the most Eastern boundary of Walton County, Florida, runs approximately 100 miles from its headwaters near Geneva, Alabama, to its terminus in the Bay by the same name. Its watershed covers over 5,000 square miles, and by volume it is the third largest river in Florida. European and white settlers have relied upon its waters for transportation, commerce, and subsistence for centuries. And before them, the "River of the Choctaw" (the literal rendering of "Choctawhatchee") did the same for the local tribe by the same name and generations of aboriginal peoples before them. It is an irreplaceable natural resource, and so are the people and stories that have populated its banks and sandbars.

All the stories in this book come directly from the Grit & Grace archives. For 15 years, the organization has been collecting folklore, historical accounts, and personal stories from the residents of Walton County and portraying them on stage. The stories here, many shorter and in a more narrative style, may not lend themselves readily to the theater, but they read like miniature memoirs (and I have left them largely intact, honoring dialect, colloquialisms, and without correcting historical inaccuracies). I hope you enjoy reading them as much as I enjoyed editing and collecting them.

A final note about this collection: A large number of these stories were first published by the Northwest Florida Water Management District a generation ago. I use the word "published" loosely, as the original book was a simple, typewritten, spiral bound notebook of sorts entitled, "Historical Remembrances of Choctawhatchee River." The stories contained within were pure gold, and worthy of a new generation's attention. They are produced here with the Northwest Florida Water Management District's full permission, and below I have included the preface to their original edition.

I hope, as you let these stories throw a little light on your past and path, that you will remember that no one would ever see a pointing finger in the first place, without the luminous moon. And a book like this one would never be possible without our history's shining people and their stories.

Ronnie McBrayer
June 2016
Freeport, Florida

HISTORICAL REMEMBRANCES
OF CHOCTAWHATCHEE RIVER

Edited by George Fisher

(1989 PREFACE)

In 1982, this District made its first attempt at gathering oral accounts of life and resource use in northwest Florida. Ten "old timers" each selected to represent an economic or subsistence activity common around the Choctawhatchee Bay during the early part of the 20th century, were interviewed and featured in a District publication. This publication, *Historical Remembrance of Choctawhatchee Bay*, proved to be one of the most popular the District has produced. It was also a very useful publication in that it provided us with insight into important conditions and attitudes concerning the bay. For example, the location of sea grass and oyster beds as they were 50 or 60 years ago, the earlier distribution of fresh and saltwater creatures, and first-person accounts of the origins of commercial fishing in the area all provided for a greater understanding of "natural" conditions in the bay while also allowing us to more fully comprehend local attitudes concerning water and wildlife resources.

The popularity and especially the usefulness of the Choctawhatchee Bay interviews contributed greatly to our decision to carry out a similar project, this time focusing on the "bottomlands," or floodplain, of the Choctawhatchee River. In this instance, we were primarily interested in interviewing individuals who had spent a lifetime on or near the river and who could help us better understand traditional uses and activities as they related to this particular floodplain. Our need for this information was more pressing than would normally be the case. This was mainly because we were in the process of planning public uses for the 35,198 acre Choctawhatchee River Water Management Area recently acquired by the District. An extremely important consideration in this planning was that, whenever possible, there should be a "continuation of local and traditional land and water resource uses." We could think of no better source for this information than to interview in depth those who had been born and raised on the river.

Out of the many dozens of people recommended as being excellent sources of information about life on the Choctawhatchee during the first decades of the century, we had to select a few that we thought could provide us with the broadest possible range of lifestyles, experiences, livelihoods, and personalities. This turned out to be extremely fortuitous; these were the most diverse and informative interview subjects we could have hoped for, and they were, without exception, tremendously interesting, entertaining, and hospitable. We greatly appreciate the cooperation and contributions of all who participated.

Northwest Florida Water Management District
Historical Remembrances of Choctawhatchee River
Water Resources Special Report 89-1
March 1989

SPECIAL REPORT CREDITS
Interviews, Compilation, Editing, and Design
George Fisher, Editor
Carla Campbell
Maria Culbertson
Lee Cobb
Kim Davis
Tom Francis
Elaine McKinnon
Tom Pratt
Jan Smith
Dianne Sterling
Thelma Whitfield
Susan Whittle

FOR EVERYBODY

By JOHNNIE MORRISON

*John Leonard "Johnnie" Morrison was born
along the Choctawhatchee River on April 23,
1903. He was a deputy sheriff for eight years; a
security guard in Texas; a private chauffeur in
West Palm Beach, Florida, and New York City,
New York; and a maintenance foreman for the
Florida Road Department.[1] Mr. Morrison died
in 1993, and is buried in the Leonia Cemetery of
Holmes County, Florida.*

I moved down south and worked in the Everglades on a dredge boat. From there I went to West Palm Beach and worked at the Police Department and then got a private chauffeur job. But I was too far away from the Choctawhatchee River every time, and I love that old river so well. I was raised on it, so I had to come back to it. I've worked among the wealthiest people in the world, and I'd rather be sitting on a log in this river swamp with $5 in my pocket than have a million dollars in New York City. And I'd rather hear one of them old hoot-owls on the river, hollering, than hear the Grand Ole Opry. I've had good opportunities everywhere, but I had to come home to my river.

I used to camp along the river. We didn't have ice or anything, so when we were thirsty we would drink right out of river. It was good. I still drink the water out of the river if I get thirsty. It's good, but not like it used to be. And when I was younger there weren't many bridges. We had to use ferryboats. And I've even seen them load up cows on the ferries and use cables to pull them across. It was pretty rough going back then, especially in high water.

The fish out of the Choctawhatchee are the best. I know, I've eaten fish out of every river in Florida, and I fished commercially for a little while after I retired. It was mostly catfish, and I could get ten cents a pound to local restaurants. For myself I used to catch bream, bass, jackfish, and shell crackers from the river. I caught a few moonshiners too!

The moonshiners used to be from one end of this river to the other. I was a deputy from 1932-40 and worked with a federal man. The bootleggers would scatter their traffic – so trails would not be visible – but the hogs and pigs would make straight trails to the stills and we could follow the hogs. They love the mash. When we would start to tear up a still, and the pigs would hear us beating on the drum, they would come running. Whiskey was $2 a gallon back then. There were some real big stills and some were as nice as kitchens. You had to catch the bootleggers by surprise. They would freeze right there if you did. But other times, as soon as they heard a stick break they were gone, just like a deer, and you were lucky if you could catch them. I chased some of them as far as the Alabama line!

But now I hunt for game – not moonshiners. There are a lot of wild hogs, but the turkey population is gone from the river swamp and the deer have taken over. I've never seen any bear, but I've heard of some being killed. We have plenty of wildcats and bobcats, but I don't believe there's any panther left. Sometime when those hoot-owls scream they can sound like a panther, though. There's beavers all over the country now. I don't believe they're good for the area because they kill so many trees. They're pests, but maybe they are as good as they are bad. And I'm not the only hunter. There's more people hunting now than when I was a boy. On hunting season morning it sounds like a war out here!

With you folks (the Northwest Florida Water Management District) buying land around the river, keep it for the enjoyment of the people, for fishing and hunting and commercial traffic.[2] It would be productive if you could mine the lime rock in there. They need to get in there and channel the river out so they can get up and down. We could have ferryboats. If the water keeps on getting flatter and flatter, we're going to have saltwater up in here. The sandbars keep piling up and pushing the river toward the coves. The timber is still there and I was proud of the State of Florida when they bought this all up and stopped the logging. It's just a beautiful scene from one end of the river to the other.

If the river could be controlled, it would be a beautiful place to live. But the river is too uncertain; it's like an elevator – up and down, up and down. But I bet in a hundred years, there will be houses all along it. I'd still want the beauty of the river preserved; the shrubs and trees, the hogs, fish and ducks. Some people just don't know when to quit catching fish and quit killing game.[3]

But there's still a river here that we can

use, though the water level is low, and in a couple of years water is going to be very valuable. I just love that river. It's such a wonderful place. And there's something else I'd like to say: It's one of the dirtiest tricks ever when somebody puts up a gate on an old road that been open a hundred years. The people who are leasing some of this land near the river to a certain few are depriving the other people of the privilege of using the river. It belongs to the State of Florida and it should be for everybody here to enjoy it.

1   George Fisher, *Historical Remembrances of Choctawhatchee River* (Havana, FL: NWFL Water Management District, 1989), 13-19.

2   The Water Resources Act of 1972, created the Northwest Florida Water Management District (NWFWMD). It is charged with managing the water resources of the Florida panhandle in a sustainable manner that benefits both people and natural resources. The district reports having acquired more than 85 percent of the floodplains along the Choctawhatchee River.

3   The NWFWMD now maintains numerous boat landings along the Choctawhatchee River, managing recreational activities that include seasonal hunting, camping, fishing, paddling, hiking, and wildlife observation.

DOWN BY THE RIVERSIDE

SNAKE BIT

By Mrs. W.H. Miller

This funny little tale was gleaned from a few faded, age-worn, handwritten pages in the bottom of a Grit & Grace shoebox. It is a treasure, transcribed by all appearances, from an oral interview. The author/storyteller is "Mrs. W.H. Miller."

***

Old Doc McKinnon from Freeport told us that once when he was called to Alaqua to doctor a sick man, his dog cornered a big rattlesnake.[4] While the snake had his attention on the pup, the doctor slipped up behind the snake and grabbed it behind the head and held it at arm's length. With his left hand he got his knife from his pocket, opened it with his teeth, and with a few fancy circles on the air clipped the snake's head from its body. If you could be quick, the doctor said, there was never any danger, though some folks were terrified of rattlesnakes.

There was such man who was traveling through this part of the country. He grew tired and stopped by a house to ask the folks if might stay the night. They said they had little, but he was welcome to stay.

After supper was over and they sat around talking, the traveler noticed a string of what looked like dried ears of popcorn and commented on it. He was told it was rattlesnake rattles as this was a snaky part of the county. The wife began to tell him all about them. One snake was killed in the field, one at the spring, one in the cow pen, and one was killed when it crawled out of an armload of firewood. She said she had killed one that very day by the chimney, and had seen its mate by the gate just before the traveler had arrived for supper.

Well, the man was frightened and knew he wouldn't sleep a wink, but when bedtime came, he was so very tired, and the family put him in a little shed room against the main house. The bed was only made of boards, but he fell asleep only to dream of rattlesnakes.

He stretched his leg out during the night and something struck his ankle with force. He knew it was a rattler and jumped out of bed to tell the family. They began in on him right away. They tied a rag around his leg near the knee and made him drink tobacco tea to throw up the poison. He wrote his wife a parting letter and drank the tea. He threw up the black poison until he was weak as water.

The people thought he might be alright, but needed to kill the snake that had bit him before anybody could go back to sleep. They went into the shed and before long called the traveler in to see the "snake." There was an old hen sitting on a flour can at the end of the traveler's bed. She was the "snake," and he had only been pecked, not snake bit.

They all went back to bed, and the traveler made sure he stayed on his side of the bed so the hen could have her room.

4 "Old Doc McKinnon" appears to be Dr. Charles Braxton McKinnon. From Harry Gardner Cutler's *History of Florida, Past and Present, Volume II* (1923): "Among the more distinguished physicians and surgeons of Walton County, who have established a reputation for ability and integrity, none are more worthy of attention than Dr. Charles B. McKinnon of DeFuniak Springs. He has not only achieved honorable success in his profession, but has gained distinction in public and military affairs, and his progressive spirit is evident in many ways... The McKinnon family originated in the Isle of Skye, Scotland, whence the early members of the families bearing this name immigrated to America, settling in the Carolinas for the most part and then moving on to the old Scotch settlement in Walton County" (137).

DOWN BY THE RIVERSIDE

AT THE YANCEY HOUSE

By Verna Hughes

Verna Hughes was the daughter of George B. Hughes and Hortie Mella Gillman. The Hughes family thrived in the communities of Walton and Holmes Counties, and continues to do so. This account, another from the Grit & Grace archive, is verified by Verna's niece, Latilda Hughes-Neel. Latilda has been a Grit & Grace volunteer in almost every capacity, and is the long-tenured Planning Director for the City of Freeport.

Parents Creek, just down the hill from the Yancey house, was a center of many occurrences of my youth. We swam in it, fished in it, and hunted squirrels and picked huckleberries in the woods that surrounded it. Long before I learned to swim, I remember going to the swimming hole upstream from the bridge, and playing around the shallow edge. Sometimes my brother Rubert would take me on his back and swim across the deep part of the swimming hole. What a thrill that was! And it was he who encouraged and finally talked me into turning lose and trying to swim to the sand bar. I did! That was my first time to swim.

Rubert was quite a fisherman. At certain times of the year, huge sucker fish would swim up the creek from the Choctawhatchee River, which was about two miles away. Those large fish could be seen lying quietly in the bottom of the creek in a deep, shadowy pool, seemingly asleep.

Using a table hook on a stout pole, he would snatch the hook into the fish's soft mouth. and the fight was on! There was a tree stump standing upright on the bank, partway in the water. The creek had eroded the bank around it until some of the roots were exposed and extended out over the water. Rubert had climbed over the stump was standing on these extended soots so he could get in a good position to snatch one. The position must have been right, because he did get his hook into one. When he did, the big fish gave a lunge and Rupert was pulled into the creek! I remember that big fish lying on the bank, still flopping around on the hook, while Rubert laid out his Prince Albert tobacco and papers on a stump to dry.

When there was lots of rain, the Choctawhatchee River would rise, and the backwater would run the creek out of its banks into the low-lying areas. This was set-hook time. Using a small boat that he had built, Rubert would put our bush-hooks, baiting them with "puppy dogs," hoping to catch channel catfish that swam in from the river. Sometimes I got to go with him to fish the set hoots. As we moved through the muddy water among the bushes, someone would look ahead and say, "Look yonder at the bush jerking!" And sure enough there would be a big white-sided channel catfish on the line, struggling to get free of the hook. As I look back, those were some of the biggest and prettiest fish I ever saw. Mama must have thought so too. She would "oooh and aaah" over them when we got home, and begin to tell how good they would be when she got them cooked.

In addition to the fishing methods already mentioned, the old tried and tested cane pole was used extensively. Earthworms were the bait that was used; I don't recall anyone using crickets at that time. Getting earthworms was easy, if one knew how to do it. We didn't dig them – we grunted or snored them out of the ground. This was accomplished by driving a wooden peg or stob into the ground some eight or ten inches, then rubbing a board or piece of metal across the top, causing vibration. The worms would come out of the ground and begin to crawl about. I recall helping pick them up, and how wet and sticky they felt. Sometimes as many as thirty or forty worms wold come up in just one grunting session.

Fishing could be painful sometimes. Out in the backyard one day, Mama and Rubert were cleaning some catfish we had caught. I was feeling one of the fish when it gave a quick flounce. I cried out in pain as one of its sharp fins thrust into my thumb. Mama rushed over and freed me of the catfish. It was very painful so Mama applied a turpentine and tallow bandage to it which helped tremendously. She would put a turpentine and tallow poultice on our chests at bed time if any of us had a cold. As I am certain my brothers and sisters will recall, there were a number of medicinal remedies that Mama administered to us.

There were Cream of Tarter and Sulphur Tablets that were supposed to be good for the blood, particularly during "Dog Days." Mama kept a flat, round, metal container of salve she used a good bit, called Petro Carbo Salve. It was about the color of motor oil and was used on burns and cuts. She also had some black

14

salve that smelled like tar. She said it would draw the swelling and soreness out of bee sting or an infected place.

In the springtime she gave us Grove's Chill Tonic. This elixir must have contained iron, which certainly would bolster up one's color, improve the appetite, and in general make us feel better. Then, if one had chills and fever, out came the Cocoa Quinine. And with all the assurances that it would make you feel better, you took it. We would begin to feel better sooner or later, and would hear the statement, "See, I told you. That medicine really works!"

Mama kept on hand a bottle of Watkin's Liniment, bought off the Rolling Store, which was as close to being the all-around medicine as you could get. It was rubbed on insect bites, wasp or bee-stings. How many cuts and bruises did Mama patch up, with words of comfort to soothe and console her injured child? And as I remembered, I became much more conscious of how important she was in our young lives, and how much she loved us, and how she sacrificed to help us have the things we needed.

DOWN BY THE RIVERSIDE

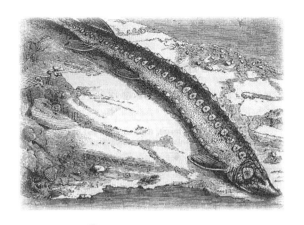

THE CHOCTAWHATCHEE BAY

By Dan Owens

For almost 20 years Dan Owens has served the people of Walton County as the Director of the Public Library System. Dan has a Bachelor of Arts in Library Science from North Texas State University, a Master of Business Administration from Golden Gate University, and a Master of Library Science degree from Emporia State University. He has served on the Advisory Council for NEBASE, which was Nebraska's regional service provider for

*the Online Computer Library Center services,
and he has served two terms on the Board of
Directors of the Panhandle Library Access
Network. He retired from the United States Air
Force after 22 years of service and considered
himself a wandering Texan before settling in
DeFuniak Springs in 1999. This is his original
poem.*

***

The only place I long to be
    As I go from sea to sea
        Is that humble home for me
            On the Choctawhatchee Bay

Greater is my delight
    When it comes into sight
        Waters sparkling oh so bright
            Of the Choctawhatchee Bay

There are times I go astray
    From that regal august bay
        You can't keep me far away
            From the Choctawhatchee Bay

Eagle, ibis, mockingbird
    Fish, crow, mallard, hummingbird
        Swallow, blue jay, all are heard
            On the Choctawhatchee Bay
Turtle, gator, fox and deer

Turkey, rabbit, snakes and bear
Raccoon, possum all draw near
To the Choctawhatchee Bay

The bounty of the bay's a wonder
Sturgeon, brim, bass and flounder
No one there to steal your thunder
On the Choctawhatchee Bay

Purest waters ever seen
Of the deepest blue and green
Floating onward in a dream
On the Choctawhatchee Bay

Just a cool refreshing breeze
Lets you do what 'er you please
While you live a life of ease
On the Choctawhatchee Bay

Matters not how far I roam
The sweetest honey on the comb
Is found in my beloved home
On the Choctawhatchee Bay

DOWN BY THE RIVERSIDE

DEADHEADING

By James Franklin "Frankie" Smith

"Frankie" Smith describes himself as a naturalist who "guides, fishes, hunts, traps, buys and sells" on the Choctawhatchee. Born in 1945, Frankie has lived along the Choctawhatchee's banks all his life except while serving in the Army Corps of Engineers. He has been a police officer, sawmill operator, and is a certified diver.[5] Mr. Smith died December 27, 2006, at his home along the Choctawhatchee River.

I've hunted, fished, and trapped; and I've taken people out on the Choctawhatchee River all my life. It's a beautiful place and I don't know why anyone calls it a "swamp." I had a sawmill and cut cypress singles by hand for most of the old "Tom Thumb" stores.

Some people talk about being hungry while living here on the river. I have never seen a hungry day in my life. My mother made the garden, we had cows and hogs for meat, and we could always go to the river for food. My family has been right here for three generations. They came here from Alabama; they were farmers and loggers but mostly grew cotton for cash and corn for livestock. The cotton gin we used was at Cerro Gordo on the river.[6] There was a jail, the gin, a grist mill, and a ferry. Now there is only a boat landing there.

It's kind of sad, because where barges used to go, you have trouble getting there now with a johnboat. Erosion is the problem, both here and north of here. There are places that always stayed ten feet deep that now are only a few inches deep. Some people say we should leave it alone, but if the river isn't dredged, we won't be able to use it for boats. It will wind up being a creek and an Alabama junkyard. You wouldn't believe the trash they throw in there. The logging operations cut the timber out, the farming changed the sediment, and now we have so much erosion. The river has just finally filled up.

"Deadheading" is gone now too; and
"Deadheaders" used to live on the river. See,
back in the 1800s, they would float big rafts
of logs down the river and some of them would
sink. You used to could make good money by
pulling these logs up out of the river.[7] They,
the Deadheaders, would use a big pole to find
them. Almost all the deadheads had an old brand
on them put there by the logger.[8] The sawmill
people paid for the logs based on the brand, and
a lot of times the loggers and sawmill people
never knew or saw each other. There was a lot
of trust back then. It might take six or eight
months for the log to float to the mill, but
the logger would be paid for however many feet
were in that branded log.

The Deadheaders would have two specially
built barges that sat side by side in the river.
They would use cable and a wench to pull the
deadheads up from the bottom. They often dove
down to hook up the cable without using any
diving gear except a pair of overalls. I can
show you areas that were deadhead ramps 30
years ago, that today are hundreds of yards
from the river now.[9] The sandbars are moving
from where they've been for years; they didn't
do that when I was a kid.

When the river started filling in, the
sturgeon started leaving this area. This was
in the 1960s. The alligator gar started leaving

23

about the same time. When I was a kid, my neighbor caught alligator gar for Sears and Roebuck. You don't really skin a gar; you chop him out. He would boil the scales to clean them and then Sears and Roebuck bought them to make buttons. A lot of the old "pearl" buttons you see are really alligator gar scales.

That neighbor also caught sturgeon. It was the ugliest fish in the Choctawhatchee River. He could get some caviar, but he mainly sold the meat. It was considered a real delicacy. They caught the gar and sturgeon with a net. Stories about alligator gar or sturgeon attacking people are bunch of junk, but they would rub against a boat. You can tell if there is a sturgeon in an area by feeling under submerged logs. If it's super smooth and grooved on the bottom side, it's from a sturgeon scratching his back.

Now, I'm not going to do much of that. I'm not going to reach into a hole and grab a moccasin. I've never heard of anyone trying to catch fish with their bare hands here, mainly because there are more snakes in the Choctawhatchee than anywhere else in the world.

Sometime ago I got a letter from a man in Pensacola saying if I sent him $100, I could hunt and fish on this land I have hunted and fished all my life. A whole lot of the land is leased now and more is heading that way. The state needs to get more of the land so everybody can go in there to enjoy it. The erosion problems

24

can be stopped by planted cypress trees, and the river north of Interstate 10 needs to be cleaned out. We have about 20 years to save the Choctawhatchee. If we don't do it, it will be a dirty, polluted junkyard instead of a wild river.

5   Fisher, *Historical Remembrances*, 43.

6   "Cerro Gordo" means "Fat Hill" in Spanish, and was the site of the first Holmes County courthouse and post office (though some records refer to the same site as "Hewett's Bluff.") In 1889 a new courthouse was built in Cerro Gordo, only to be moved to Westville five years later. Within a decade that courthouse had burned, and the county seat moved to Bonifay in 1905.

7   Deadhead logs appear to get their name as a type of warning. "Dead ahead!" would come the call of the boat hands to their captain, warning of logs or debris ahead. It is estimated that ten percent of the virgin cypress logs cut for timber in the previous centuries, are at the bottom of the Florida Panhandle's rivers. Their removal is highly regulated by the State of Florida, and extremely dangerous for divers. Some consider it worth the risk, as the ancient cypress, preserved by minerals of the water, are worth their weight in gold to artisans and craftsmen.

8   Deadheads pulled from the rivers, under Florida law, could theoretically be reclaimed by the original companies that cut the timber. Almost all that are retrieved are "branded" or marked. For example, the McCaskill Timber Company of Walton County, had some two dozen logging crews working their acreage. Each crew used a different "brand" for identification purposes.

9   Deadhead logging has had a sporadic history in Florida. Before 1974, deadheading was allowed by lease and permit. In 1974, a moratorium was placed on all such activities. In 1998, the practice was once again permitted, and since then, some 25,000 logs have been retrieved from Florida waterways.

DOWN BY THE RIVERSIDE

SHEEP AND SHEPHERDS

By DANIEL W. PADGETT

Daniel Walton Padgett was born on January 30, 1927. Before his death in January 2013, he worked with special needs adults and was an ordained Baptist minister, a shepherding force touching many lives throughout Walton and Holmes Counties and beyond.[10]

27

My maternal grandfather, John Brownell, was Scottish and an expert in the making of turpentine and moonshine. He had a farm with sheep, horses, cattle, hogs, corn, and other grains. He had a shepherd dog he used in bringing in the cattle and the sheep. With open range, the animals roamed the countryside. They would spend four or five weeks shearing and marking sheep. My granddaddy had 14 children and each had his or her special marking on the ears of the sheep. When they sheared the sheep, they would put the code on the tally sheet hanging on the wall, and then they would divide up the money when they sold the wool. They had big wool sacks which must have been eight feet deep, and they would pack the wool in them. We grandsons would try to pack the wool in, and sometimes we would sink down to near the bottom of the sack and would need assistance to get out.

The wool was taken by wagon to DeFuniak Springs. I'm not sure where it went from there. Sometimes there were black sheep mixed in with the white, and they would bag the black wool in separate bags. The sheep shearing was the most interesting aspect in my memories of my grandparents. They would lay the sheep on a bench, tie the sheep's feet, and then shear them on one side with clippers; then flip the sheep over and shear the other side. They did this every year. When my grandfather died in the early 1940s, all that came to an end.

There was no industry around here at all, then. Eventually, the railroad did come in, and my father, Dan M. Padgett, was an engineer on the railroad. When he was still a teenager he became a fireman on the steam engine that came from Geneva through Ponce de Leon and on to Freeport. They laid the railroad and loaded the virgin long-leaf and yellow pine and took it to the Geneva Lumber Company. They would usually cut off the section of the tree that had been turpentined and use it for firewood. We called it "lighter." They would use teams of oxen, ten yokes of oxen, with eight oxen in each yoke, and they would pull the logs to the railroad cars. That was quite a scene.

Imagine men having to cut all those trees with crosscut saws. And they didn't cut the trees close to the ground. They cut them about waist high so they wouldn't have to bend over. They had thousands of men working, but about 1925 or so, the mill at Geneva closed up and they quit bringing the logs in. There was also the turpentine during this period. Before the railroad my grandfather would take his turpentine down to the Choctawhatchee and load it on the steamboats to send to Pensacola. When the railroads came, I think the turpentine was sent by rail to Jacksonville.

Turpentining was about like moonshining. They started with little aluminum cans that were nailed to the trees. The tree was "tapped" and the resin would run into the can. They started at the base of the tree "hacking" or pulling a strip of bark off the tree. The "hacking" would sometimes reach as high as eight to ten feet over the years. It would take a few weeks to fill the containers, and a dipper would be used to empty the individual cans into a bucket, and then barrels. When I was a boy they let me drive the mule and wagon with the barrels. This was a lot of fun.

The woods were not as thick with undergrowth as they are now because the woods were burned every year and the cows would eat the vegetation. You could see long distances, and this prevented fire from destroying the turpentine trees. So, the turpentine wagons went to the stills to produce mineral spirits. They boiled the resin down and cooled it through an evaporation process.

After the lumber and turpentine business played out, World War II was brewing and the Eglin Field was beginning to develop.[11] Many people went down there to help clear out that wilderness. People worked in Eglin Field and Tyndall Field in Panama City.[12] Many people moved to those areas from here after the war. These were poor people, and farming was not profitable. The only time they had shoes was in the winter. The moonshine business helped provide food for their families, and had it not

been for moonshine, things would have been much
worse. They used to ship moonshine from here to
Chicago in medicine bottles on the railroad.

But back to the river, the riverboats had
passed away by the time I was born. The railroad
and Route 90 ended that business.[13] It was quite
active, though, along the river, because cotton
was being sent to Geneva. It was a blessing
when the boll weevil came through because it
made the farmers diversify and not depend upon
cotton. Cotton was king in those days, but the
boats carried lumber and turpentine as well.
The riverboats were good transportation too.
They traveled to Freeport, to Cerro Gordo, and
up to Geneva. Cerro Gordo, along the river, was
the Holmes County seat. My great-grandfather,
Daniel Brownell, was sheriff there in 1882, and
got into a duel. Both men were killed.[14]

The last paddleboat to navigate the river
was the "Fritz."[15] My Aunt Annie Wells went
aboard it one time when the river was low and
they had a long plank from the boat to the
docking ramp to walk on board. She made her
brother hold her hand when she walked across.
Evidently, it would have been quite a scene to
see the paddle wheels going up and down the
river. They were necessary for the commercial
trade before the railroad came.

The river is changing its course quite a bit
- especially at Cerro Gordo, and they say that
the actual site of the old courthouse is now on

the other side of the river from where it was originally. The river is cutting in a westerly direction because you can see where the curves are, and how the erosion is taking place along the west bank. Back when I was a boy, you never saw the water as low as you do now. Maybe it's caused by the lack of rain, but the creeks that used to run into the river were never dry.

I don't think the river should be dredged. I believe it would be better off just like it is. It's really not a river for big boats. It's more for fishing and wildlife. Boats just make a mess anyway when they throw their garbage in the water. The best thing I believe is to let the river be natural. Let it take its natural course.

10 Fisher, *Historical Remembrances*, 21.

11 The Valparaiso Bombing and Gunnery Base was activated June 1935. On August 4, 1937, the base was re-designated Eglin Field in honor of Lieutenant Colonel Frederick I. Eglin, an Air Corps officer killed in an aircraft crash earlier that same year.

12 Tyndall Field opened in January 1941 as a gunnery range. The airfield was named in honor of Lieutenant Frank Benjamin Tyndall (1894–1930). Tyndall, a World War I pilot and Silver Star recipient, was killed in a routine inspection flight.

13 In 1883, the Louisville & Nashville Railroad completed the rail link from Pensacola to Chattahoochee, Florida. Route 90, which passes through the county seats of all 15 counties in North Florida, was first designated a US Highway in 1925.

14 "Cerro Gordo" means "Fat Hill" in Spanish, and was the site of the first Holmes County courthouse and post office (though some records refer to the same site as "Hewett's Bluff.") In 1889 a new courthouse was built in Cerro Gordo, only to be moved to Westville five years later. Within a decade that courthouse had burned, and the county seat moved to Bonifay in 1905.

15 The "Captain Fritz" was a 57-ton steamer built in 1892. The last of the paddle wheeled boats on the Choctawhatchee River, it measured 99 by 22 feet. The Fritz gave the river a record 38 years of service.

DOWN BY THE RIVERSIDE

SCULLS AND SKITTERS

By BARZILLA AND ADDIE GOMILLION

Mr. and Mrs. Gomillion were both born in the Red Bay community. Mrs. Addie (nee Lassiter) was born in 1912, and Mr. "B." in 1900. He helped build railroads and bridges for most of his life, and she was a dedicated homemaker who raised five children. Both of the Gomillions claim their hobby is to "sit at home and look at each other and grumble and growl."[16] Addie died not long after this interview was completed (1989). Mr. "B." died May 3, 1993, in DeFuniak Springs.

The older folks, like our parents, drifted logs down the river. When the water was down they would go to the swamp and cut the trees, and when the water was up, they'd tie 'em up and take them to Freeport. It was called a "log drive." And you used to be able to go and catch a mess of fish and be back home in three hours. There ain't no fish in the Choctawhatchee River now. They're gone!

We always turkey hunted and squirrel hunted. And the wood ducks were some of the best eating in the world. But you can't get them. You see, these companies have come in and cut all the oak trees and everything and there's nothing for animals to eat. They got all the land leased around here. There's a sign that says, "Keep Out! No Hunting Allowed!" Some places even have wires and chains to keep people out. We used to trap and sell coon hides for $11 a piece – and an otter hide brought $35! Not anymore.

But we could at least live. We had 40 acres and we made what we ate except for the flour and stuff like that. We grew corn, peanuts, and cotton. We even had hogs down in the swamp. And we remember the riverboat trade. The "Fritz" was at the Miller place when it burned. It was a big boat and blew the loudest horn you ever heard. I think J.D. Sharron was the captain, but I don't know who was the captain of another boat called the "Bruce." I think it burned in the Bay.

Anyhow, these riverboats were used for hauling freight. Hauling whatever needed to be hauled, I guess. There were no big trucks then, and everything went by water. It would come from Pensacola and go up to Geneva and back. The riverboat landings were at Miller's and Wise Bluff and they carried passengers too. It was transportation to Pensacola and back. We also used our own boat. It was a scull boat − we had to put an oar in a slot in the back of the boat and scull on down the river. When the boats with motors started coming, that's when we quit that.

Eventually, the railroad took over some of the transportation. Geneva Mill Logging Company used to have a railroad through these woods when they were cutting timber.[7] I was 12-years old when I worked at Geneva Mills, helping them lay steel. They transferred me down to Freeport and I helped build railroads all across this area. This was about 1921. You see, the timber was cut in the woods and it was "snaked" to the railroad with oxen and mules. They'd load the logs on the flat-cars and carry them in. "Skitters" are those machines with the motor that pulls the logs. They had mules pulling a cable going back into the woods. They'd hook up the logs and then the skitter would pull the logs in to be loaded. The mules would come back and get the skitter line and carry it back into the woods.

For our grandchildren, we'd like the river to be dredged, that way there'd be room for boats to go up, and a bridge for them to go under, like they used to when we went to Geneva. The river's filled up with dirt and old tree tops and stumps and things. That would sure help the fishing too, I believe. The game wardens would tell you there's plenty of fish in the Choctawhatchee River, but when you go fishing and stay all day and don't catch a mess of fish, you know there aren't many fish.

The river is an important thing, and the prettiest place I know is around Rooks Bluff.[18] That's about two miles below Bruce. It's a beautiful place down there.

16 Fisher, *Historical Remembrances*, 7.

17 In the first two decades of the 20th Century, the Geneva Mill Company had miles of logging railroads in Walton County and a mill at Freeport with capacity of 50,000 feet.

18 Rooks Bluff is accessible today via Black Creek Road (Walton County Road 3280). A boat ramp is maintained in that location by the Florida Fish and Wildlife Conservation Commission.

DOWN BY THE RIVERSIDE

TUPELO

By Ronnie McBrayer

In the winter of 2015, I was attending a community seminar at the meeting house of the Muscogee Nation of Florida (278 Church Road, Bruce, Florida 32455). The Muscogee, also known as the Florida Tribe of Eastern Creek Indians, are a proud tribe from primordial towns that existed as part of the Creek Confederacy in the Southeastern United States before the nineteenth century. Serendipitously, I meet Kenna Pate at that meeting, a member of the Muscogee Tribe and a lifelong beekeeper. Our conversation, and his wealth of knowledge, inspired the song below.

Ask any group of people where "Tupelo Honey" comes from and many will respond, "Mississippi." But that's the wrong answer. Tupelo, Mississippi has black gum trees, but that region of the South does not produce Tupelo Honey.

Tupelo Honey is produced from the pollination of the nyssa ogeche – the Ogeechee Tupelo – which flowers in the spring and ripens in the fall. Ogeechee Tupelo only grow in the swampy soil of the Southeastern United States, from coastal South Carolina through the Ogeechee Valley in Georgia to the Florida Panhandle. And it is only North Florida, from the lower Choctawhatchee River in the west to the Apalachicola River in the east, that the most pure and highly graded Tupelo Honey is produced.

Tupelo Honey is especially light and sweet, so high in fructose that it will not crystallize or spoil. Thus, it is in high demand, a demand intensified by the nyssa ogeche's short flowering season. Beekeepers must move their hives near the groves of Tupelo trees for only three to five short weeks. After that, a full year will pass before the trees bloom and Tupelo Honey production can begin again. This production now exceeds $1 million annually in sales, a significant agricultural boost for Walton County and the surrounding area.

The original song below was written specifically for the 2016 presentation of Grit & Grace, again, under the tutelage of Kenna

42

Pate, a lifelong resident of Walton County and beekeeper along the Choctawhatchee River.

"TUPELO"

CHORUS
Bring me that honey, Tupelo;
Jar up that nectar from the comb.
That's the taste, clear and sweet;
Best in the world, it can't be beat,
Bring me that honey, Tupelo!

VERSE 1
I hear the talk that's going round;
Where the sweetest honey can be found.
It's not down in Mississip';
Caroline or the Georgia Pines.
But right here in my Walton County home!

VERSE 2
Down on that Choctaw River shore;
The bees are buzzing, Lord, galore!
Buildin' those hives, grabbin' that gum;
That's where the best comes from.
Right here in my Walton County home!

VERSE 3
I sure don't mean to cause offense;
To the keepers on the other side of the fence.
But what they call, "Tupelo,"
Is just a fraud that can't be sold;
If it's not from my Walton County home!

43

DOWN BY THE RIVERSIDE

nine

MONDAY TO MONDAY

By Albert "Jabot" Williams

Albert "Jabot" Williams was born in the second decade of the twentieth century, "about two miles from the the Choctawhatchee River." He indicates that he has never lived further than that from the river. As a youngster, he tended large numbers of hogs that roamed the Choctawhatchee floodplain. He also briefly tried making moonshine, and as was locally famous for being one of the fastest runners afoot.[19]

There was plenty of good timber when I was young. The timber companies didn't clean the forest out, they just cut the biggest and the best. When they were done, there was still a good stand of timber left. But when the paper company got hold of it, they started cleaning it out.[20] They used to run the logs down the river to Freeport. Then they put that big mill in Caryville that Brown Florida Lumber Company owned.[21] They filled up the river with so many logs that the fish couldn't swim.

And people don't swim in the Choctawhatchee like they used to. Once in a while you'll see young people swimming down by a boat ramp, but not often. When I was younger, it was about the only place we had to go swimming. Back in the 1930s, the water at the boat ramp used to be from eight to 20 feet deep. Now, when it's low, I can get in it and wade for two miles. It didn't start filling up so bad until the 1940s.

I couldn't tell you how much I've fished the river. When I was a boy, I used to fish about every day. Me and my mama was raising hogs in the swamp. I stayed there looking after the hogs and the cows and the fish. Sometimes I would get some bait and stay out there all night. It was open swamp back then. There was no undergrowth because the big timber kept it down. Me and my mama had over 200 head of hogs in there, and they'd stay fat. Alabamians would come down here ever year and buy our hogs. Back in the

1930s, when times was hard, we'd live on $100 a year. Me and mother, we'd sell from $100 to $500 worth of hogs a year and be okay.

I remember that old man Warren Commander lived on the river bridge.[22] It was an old, wooden bridge – a drawbridge. Mr. Commander and his wife lived in a house attached to that bridge. He tended it and watched the river. I don't think there was ever a boat big enough come through that he had to turn it. A lot of people had little farms. That was before the paper mill came in. People have changed. Back when I was a boy, people were more neighborly. If somebody was sick, they'd walk four or five miles to sit up with them. They don't do that any more.

Another memory is when the "Old Hag Show" came through – there were about 15 wagons. I went to see their elephants cross the river. There were two big elephants. One was named Mary, the other one was Jim.[23] The Old Spanish Trail went down to the river to the ferry. But the elephants didn't cross it. They couldn't be put on it, and the wagons bogged down, anyway. So they walked them across. The water came over the top of them, and they would stick their old snouts up as high as they could get them. They set up their show in Caryville, DeFuniak, Bonifay, Pensacola, and bigger places. Then they started shipping them on trains.

There's a shortage of moonshine now, but

it used to be the biggest money crop in this county. Just about everybody around here made it. It was a joke that some people wore badges to keep everybody else from selling them shine! I operated a still a little while but never got caught at it. They couldn't catch me. I just flat out ran the revenuers. I used to be the fastest man around here. I ran right alongside a GMC pickup truck doing 35 miles per hour. If the law ever recognized who it was, they quit chasing me. They didn't want to race.

But I only made moonshine for a little while, because I drank up my profit. One time I made five gallons of good, strong whiskey. I'd say it was 100 proof. I sold three pints on a Monday morning and went to drinking what I had left until the next Monday. I stayed drunk for a week and just about dead for another – it liked to have killed me. Four gallons and a pint will kill anybody in a week, so I quit fooling with it. But this river's all good to me. I just love to be out here.

19 Fisher, *Historical Remembrances*, 71.

20 In the 1880s, much of the Florida Panhandle was covered with virgin longleaf pine forests, the likes of which no one will ever see again. By 1930, virtually all of these trees had been clearcut.

21 The Brown-Florida Lumber Company incorporated on December 5, 1925. It dissolved in late 1939.

22 A 1900 census lists a D. Warren and Lizzie Commander homesteading in Walton County. In October 1912, the Commanders sold the land to Lizzie's brother, and by 1930, Warren worked for the state of Florida as the keeper of the toll bridge near Westville.

23 It's almost impossible to know for certain which traveling circus Mr. Williams alludes to here. It's not beyond speculation to conclude that this is the "Sparks Circus," a traveling show that toured the South from the 1890s until the 1930s. Per Mr. Williams' remembrances, Sparks had a 15 wagon show and featured an Asian elephant named Mary. Mary was publicly and horrifically executed in Erwin, Tennessee, after she killed a handler. Charlie Sparks, the show's founder, morbidly employed an improvised gallows - a 100-ton crane used to lift railway cars off the tracks - to hang her.

DOWN BY THE RIVERSIDE

OF HIGH LIFE AND HOBOS

By Phyllis Douglass Dawson

Phyllis Frazier Douglass Dawson was the daughter of Angus Gillis Douglass and Laura Scott McConnell Douglass. Her 1940 Walton High School Yearbook lists her accomplishments as "senior class president, editor of the yearbook, Halloween Queen, homeroom president, solo cornet for the band, and 'substitute football player.'" In fact, Phyllis was the first female in Florida history to play in a high school football game. Coach Ox Clark put her in the game versus Blountstown on October 27, 1939, to kick an extra point, a play that was picked up and reported by the Associated Press (Ironically, her son Scott would become an NFL referee).[24] She married Archibald Nail Dawson, Jr., a decorated Navy fighter pilot who saw two Pacific tours of duty during World War II. The transcribed interview below is from the early 2000s shortly before her death. She and her husband are buried in the Magnolia Cemetery.

***

There's been a lot of insanity in this place, I tell you. This is a bird sanctuary for people. Well, now see, that would be the name of my book, "The Bird Sanctuary." That's what I would name it because we're all birds here. Just a bunch of crazy things. Like gypsies, tramps, and hobos. This town was full of hobos.

Some of them hobos stayed, but most were always en route. And we have fed many of them at our back door. And that's always been sort of interesting to me. They survived the Depression by taking trains town to town. They weren't robbers or thieves. Oh, my mother had a remedy for thieves.

Jasper would drive mama and us to North Carolina for the summer, but there were all kinds of things packed in the mountains around Birmingham, Alabama. It would take a day just to get through Birmingham with all the climbing you had to do. And the cars wouldn't go very fast.[25] Before we would leave on this trip, you couldn't even go in the house. Your eyes would burn so bad. She would concoct this mess on the stove that would be red pepper and kerosene and everything you could think of that would burn, "High Life", and all that stuff and she would put it in a flip gun. Now, I don't know if anybody's seen a flip gun lately. You could pump it and it would spray.[26]

Well, she kept that flip gun in her pockets, the big, elastic pockets in her dress, and she had a sharp butcher knife in there. Well, when you go up though the mountains, you're going about 20 miles an hour or slower. Robbers would be in those mountains and jump on your running boards and take your car or kill you or something else. Well my mother was ready! She had that flip gun there and I'm telling you she would have killed a person by spraying them, though she never had occasion to use it. But she had it ready! She was a funny, feisty thing from Charleston with the cutest accent you ever heard.

Anyways, hobos weren't to be afraid of, and DeFuniak was a good place for hobos. They would never come to your front door or come after dark. They would ask for work, not food. Those people who were marked favorably usually had a garden or something like a broken fence or wood to be chopped to give the hobo work. In exchange they would be given food, pies, or fruit to eat or take with them. The hobo always had his own cup, jar, and plate with necessary utensils in that little pack or in his overalls pocket. The hobo was self-prepared.

Hobos had good songs and great stories they shared together and with others when valued. They were polite and sometimes, as I said, a hobo might stay. We have several who came and stayed in Walton County. Hobos were great cooks - they were the original hamburger stretchers. They could stew a squirrel, filet a rabbit, or strip a snake. How to stretch soup was their specialty. Now, I would have been leery of their cooked frogs, lizards, and possums. Though their sweet potatoes were probably good. The sights of a hobo campfire where songs, stories, and good smells that were probably assisted by a little moonshine. There was plenty of it in Walton County.

As related to me by my grandmother, hobos had been field hands, railroad workers, fisherman, and many other things. They had names like Broadway Bill, Packer, Slim, Hot Sauce, and Fuzzy. Most were good singers too, because they had lived through so much. Hobos were welcomed because people here suffered together and shared whatever they had with others - they still do.

24 Bob D'Angelo, *Never Fear: The Life and Times of Forest K. Ferguson, Jr.* (Tampa: D'Angelo, 2015), 77-81.

25 Ms. Dawson is referring to the late 1920s or early 1930s. Cars produced on average only about 25 horsepower.

26 "High Life," a common household chemical from the early 20th Century, was actually carbon disulfide. Because of its poisonous, highly flammable nature, it fell out of regular use.

DOWN BY THE RIVERSIDE

HERE COMES THE JUDGE

By E. W. "Judge" Carswell

E.W. Carswell, better known as "Judge," was born in 1916, in Holmes County, Florida. He spent his entire adult life researching, writing about, and celebrating the traditional life of the Florida Panhandle. A proud graduate of Louisiana Technical University, Carswell wrote fifteen books and countless articles that document the history, culture, and heritage of his native state. In his lifetime he chaired five different historical societies; founded local celebrations of traditional life that included the Wausau Possum Festival and the Ponce de Leon Collard Festival; and was the recipient of over twenty awards for his writing and conservation efforts, including the

Florida Folk Heritage Award. He gave frequent lectures on north Florida folklife and heritage, was a recognized authority on Floridiana in his region, and served as the mayor of Chipley for multiple terms.[27]

***

A lot of the people living on the Choctawhatchee River are different than those who live in the uplands. These people were isolated in the early days. Those who went down to the flats had motivations other than farming. There was no industry to speak of; it was mostly a subsistence existence. They did a variety of things: Timbering, floating logs down the river, some turpentining, hunting, and gopher catching. By way of poling a barge, they would carry the gophers down to Pensacola. Nearly all the boats had gopher boxes on them. There was no refrigeration and gophers could live for weeks without food or water. Sailors liked to take them to sea as a source of fresh meat. In the 1950s, after we had exhausted our supply around here, the demand for gophers continued so that they were trucked to Pensacola from central Florida. The last gopher market in Pensacola closed around 1970.[28]

Along with gophers they would carry honey, beeswax, skins, and other produce to trade for what they needed on the frontier. Several things opened up this frontier: The railroad, compulsory school attendance, and after World War II, jobs. The younger generations have been assimilated, but there are several older folks who know the ways of the river.

Interesting enough, the Choctawhatchee basin was the last stronghold for the Carolina Parakeet. People would shoot one and the rest of the birds could come help it; they would be shot until all were killed. That characterizes this area. We shot the last duck, the last turkey, the last whatever, so that when I was a boy there were no deer or turkey in this whole area. Thankfully, both have been brought back today. That river has been a treasure for hunting and fishing, and a habitat for wildlife.[29]

At one time there was quite a lively sturgeon fishery on the river. That ended about 1930 or 1935. It was basically for the caviar, but they shipped the meat too. They were caught from the bay all the way up to Geneva.[30] A few people even made a livelihood out of catching those fish. The other fish out of the lower Choctawhatchee are wonderful tasting. The reason for that is the lower river is fed by a tremendous number of fresh springs.

Of course, there used to be steam boating on the river. I believe it was 1833 when the government set out to make the river more navigable by pulling snags out and doing some dredging. It wasn't very successful, but people all along the river used it for floating logs and for communications with Pensacola. This continued until the 1840s when the little steamboats came in. I can remember steamboats still running up to Geneva until about 1930, long after the railroad came along.

There's also the moonshining I want to touch on. A lot of our people, particularly those that are Scottish and Scott-Irish, had a reputation for making very good whiskey. We had local prohibition here since about 1899. That fueled the making of moonshine and it became a great industry. Timber was playing out, boll weevils were playing havoc with cotton, turpentining had seen its day and people were looking for livelihood. So people along the Choctawhatchee went in the business. There were no real large operations, just small ones that could be moved or hidden easily.

This whiskey went all over the country, and nearly all of the whiskey making took place down near the river. It was a good place to get killed too. We had an awful lot of violence with a surprisingly large number of murders each year, especially along the river. Many got away with murder because they claimed self-defense. Even after repeal of national prohibition, bootlegging continued for a long time.

And let me say one last thing about my remembrance of flooding on the Choctawhatchee. The one in 1929 was probably the worst we ever had. I got over to Caryville and watched the water. There was a bad one in 1865 they called the "Lincoln Flood," just to blame it on somebody I guess. There was a good one in 1927 caused by a hurricane; and one on July 4, 1916, that always was referred to as the "July Flood." They got 35 inches of rain from a Wednesday to the next Tuesday. It floated a steamboat right out into a cornfield and there were so many frogs people thought it had started to rain frogs instead of water.

I would like to see the Choctawhatchee area restored to what it once was. It would be a great wetlands habitat, but it would have to be protected so it could be productive.

27 Fisher, *Historical Remembrances*, 1-6.

28 The edible gopher had a long history in the Florida Panhandle. A historian from the early 1800s wrote of Pensacola: "A stream of fresh water runs through the town, and its market is well supplied with beef, garden vegetables and fish. Oysters, turtles, and gophers are important items in the supplies of food." Timothy Flint, *The History and Geography of the Mississippi Valley, Second Edition* (Cincinnati: Lincoln Press, 1832), 209.

29 The Carolina Parakeet was one of North America's only tropical parrots. The last confirmed sighting of the bird in the wild was made in 1910, and the last of the species died at the Cincinnati Zoo in 1918. The Carolina Parakeet was declared extinct in 1939.

30 The species found in the Choctawhatchee River is the Gulf Sturgeon. The fish are protected by both state and federal regulation per the Endangered Species Act. No person shall take, possess or sell any sturgeon or parts thereof, or their nests or eggs. People who inadvertently catch one have to immediately release it alive back to the water. Sturgeon can reach 10 to 12 feet in length, weigh hundreds of pounds, and live to be over 40 years old.

DOWN BY THE RIVERSIDE

DEFUNIAK LAKE

By Wallace Bruce

DeFuniak Lake is not the Choctawhatchee River, but it is a beautiful body of water nonetheless. Wallace Bruce, inspired by its beauty, wrote the short poem below.

***

Wallace Bruce was a poet, writer, lecturer, and tireless traveler. Born in Hillsdale, New York, in 1844, where the state borders both Massachusetts and Connecticut, Bruce went on to graduate from Yale, tour Europe, become an esteemed book reviewer, and eventually be

63

appointed United States consul to Edinburgh, Scotland (Of Scottish descent himself, he relished the appointment). In addition to his residence in Scotland, he maintained a home in New York, and a cottage in DeFuniak Springs, Florida.

In Walton County he would become one of the leading Florida Chautauquans, Chautauqua being that unique, American renaissance movement of the late 19th and early 20th century. Bruce succeeded W. D. Chipley as President of the Florida Chautauqua Association and held the position until his death in 1914 (except for the time his consulate appointment took him to Scotland). During his tenure the Florida Chautauqua experienced its golden years. It's programing was extensive, the historic "Hall of Brotherhood" was constructed (completed in 1909 at a cost of some $30,000), and critics concluded that the Florida Chautauqua was second in success only to the original Chautauqua Institute in New York.

Wallace Bruce's home is located on the DeFuniak Springs lake yard at 404 Circle Drive. Completed in 1888, it is known as the "Dream Cottage," and is a fine example of Folk Victorian architecture. Bruce's son, Kenneth, built his own home on the lake (circa 1907), at 550 Circle Drive, a classic Southern mansion that is a favorite of photographers. Perhaps, on the porch of one these homes, Wallace Bruce drew his inspiration.

DEFUNIAK LAKE

A Lotus Land where time forgets its date,
    A drawing place beneath the swaying trees;
        A lake so pure it seems the wedded mate,
            Of you fair sky, before the rustling breeze.

To rippling laughter wakes its gentle breast,
    Showing, it too is human.
        Oh what joy to roam in sunlight here,
            Kind nature's guest wooing her smile!

Bliss without alloy, to watch the moonlight,
    Kiss the lapsing wave;
        With one we love, and speak with answering eyes,
        The language Paradise ne'er lost,
                But gave lest man should be an outcast from
                the skies.

No spot so sweet; no water half so blue;
    God's crowning circle wrought with compass true.

DOWN BY THE RIVERSIDE

THE HOG KILLING

By John Hughes

"Let's Move to Flerdy" is a magnificent, little book of family history written in the late 1980s by John Hughes. It is a retelling of the lives and descendants of Ambrose and Amanda (nee Ellis) Gillman, Mr. Hughes' great-grandparents. Hughes' record of his great-grandfather's Civil War service makes the book worth reading, and it was the war that eventually led to the young family relocating to Holmes County and the surrounding communities. John writes, "Conditions in Dale County (Alabama) immediately following the close of the Civil War were anything but good.

*One day in the spring of 1869, Grandpa Am
had gone to Geneva, Alabama, and met up with
Grandma Mandy's brother, Bill Ellis. Bill told
him about some mighty good farm land down
where he was living. Grandpa Am related this
to his wife when he got home. That night after
supper, Grandma Mandy said, 'Am, we've had
it here. Let's move to Flerdy.'" Within days all
their earthly belongings were loaded on an ox
cart and they moved to the Florida Panhandle.
At the time of this writing, John Hughes still
makes his home here in "Flerdy." His daughter
is Latilda Hughes-Neel.*

***

A few days after New Year's, Grandpa Am
was anxious to get his hog killing done.
However, the weather had been unseasonably
warm, certainly too much so for this job. But
after a dark night of rain, the wind changed
and was coming out of the Northwest, and it
was getting colder by the hour. Grandpa made
preparations for this once-a-year job. Wood
to fire the syrup kettle was piled near it.
The smokehouse had been cleaned out and made
ready. Plenty of hickory wood was cut and
available for meat smoking. Six barrels were
clean and ready.[31]

For weeks Grandpa had been fattening the
hogs. There were eleven head, all round as

butterballs, ready to butcher. Grandpa had had mighty good luck with this litter of pigs. There had been fourteen pigs to begin with, and he had been able to raise eleven of them. Fourteen pigs in one litter was almost unheard of, and Grandpa was indeed very proud of them.

The neighbors began arriving early to help with the task at hand. One had brought his own catch dog and got busy in the rail pen. Another was getting the fire started under the syrup kettle, preparing to scald the hides of the hogs so they could be scraped and cleaned. Two long tables were being set up, using some rough lumber laid across some saw-horses cut at angles to one another.

By mid-morning the butchering process was well underway. Six of the hogs were already hanging head-down, gleaming white, from the scaffold. The men were working steadily, some scalding at the syrup kettle, while others were scraping and cleaning, getting ready to put the remaining ones on the scaffold.

The ladies present were up to their elbows in fresh pork. Some were busy cutting up fat into small pieces to be cooked out in the big wash pot. Others were cutting up lean portions of meat into small strips and bits, which would be ground into sausage. Grandma and another lady were working on the chitlins. These were carefully cut into workable lengths and emptied of their contents. Then they were washed, turned inside out, washed again, and then cleaned carefully.

The hogs were eventually cooled and placed on the long table and cut up. Each cut of meat received a "bear-grass loop" if it was to be hung in the smokehouse for smoking. The other parts – aside from what was to be made into sausage – was ready for pickling. This was accomplished by storing the pork in a barrel. First, a layer of green pine tops was placed in the barrel; then a layer of meat. Next came a layer of rock salt, then another layer of pine tops, etc., until the barrel was full. It was then closed, and rolled to a place where it would remain dry and cool until needed.

Hog-killing time was a time of both work and play for the children. There were some jobs that they could do, such as getting pine tops for the pickling, getting additional wood for the syrup kettle and wash pot, and helping prepare dinner for everybody. And still they had time to play some too.

At the end of the day, the hog-killing had been completed. After supper, Grandpa Am went out and checked the smokehouse, making sure there was enough wood to last through the night. As he and Grandma were sitting by the fireplace, he says, "Mandy, I don't know of anywhere I'd rather be than here where we live. There ain't nobody that's got better neighbors than we have. It's just a good place to live that we're at."

Grandma nodded her head in agreement as she moved gently in her rocking chair, but didn't comment. Without a doubt she must have been remembering some mighty tough times they had experienced in the past, and was also feeling very thankful for the home and fine neighbors they had.

Such were some of the day-to-day living experiences of this hardy breed of pioneers that settled this area. Without a doubt there were larger communities, and richer ones; however, the writer has doubts about any other being more loving and caring, where the people were more dedicated to each other. It is through the fabric of this community, and thousands more like it, that this great nation came to be what it is today.

31 This story, strange as it may seem to some, resonated with me. As a child I observed the last "hog killing" that my extended family ever carried out. Though a century and 400 miles separated the two events, my experience was exactly as John Hughes, using his Grandma Mandy's words, describes here. - Ronnie McBrayer

DOWN BY THE RIVERSIDE

SALT OF THE EARTH

By Donald Percy Simmons

Donald Percy Simmons was born in Point Washington on June 18, 1925. He was raised in Cowford on the banks of the Choctawhatchee River, and spent his entire life in Walton and Bay Counties. He was a World War II veteran, owner and operator of McCall's Sod Farm, and the founder of Simmons Realty. A member of the Hiland Park United Methodist Church, Mr. Simmons died on Christmas Day, 2000.

I have noticed the sands in the river have shifted during my lifetime. I have not observed a remarkable change in water quality. As a boy, I remember the cutting of timber and vegetation along the river. There was once a clear field cut all the way down to the water. The vegatation has since recovered – but not some of the beautiful, old oaks I used to see.

I was five years old when my family moved to Cowford on the Choctawhatchee River. Vernon, Hinson Crossroads, Ebro, Bruce, and Freeport – they were all there when I was growing up.[32] And when growing up I remember hearing that one of the paper companies had turned a panther lose on their property to control wild hogs which were destroying the young pine seedlings that had been planted. I saw a panther myself in 1963 on the east side of the Choctawhatchee River on Highway 20. It was around 3:00 in the morning and the panther was just standing on the side of the road.[33]

I also remember it being said that bounties were placed on eagles because they were killing so many sheep in the area. And I remember there was a stand of red oaks where a man used to whip bears out of his field with a cow whip. I have not seen any bear myself along the river. I have seen alligators and hunted them. Sometimes we would stay up all night long fishing for catfish and hunting gators to sell.

From what I remember growing up on the river, I would say that the people were just "salt of the earth" hardworking folks who raised their food by planting backyard, kitchen gardens or having little bitty farms. Some people kept loose hogs in the woods so the hogs could forage for acorns. Those hogs were not to be confused with the wild hogs that ran loose along the wilder part of the river. People would round up these hogs at night, or at least attempt to pen them up at night.

Some of the people worked in the PWA, some in the sawmills, and some in logging operations.[34] They were a very proud people, most of whom took care of their own. When someone was in need, they all would share what they had. It is true that some dabbled in the moonshine trade, but they were always the type of people who stood ready to help those among them in need. I once remember that a well-known school principal resigned his job with the school system to devote more time to his moonshine operation.

The turpentine business and logging on the river was about gone when I came along.[35] I do remember as a young boy an instance when the pilings for the Destin Bridge were drifted down the river. The pilings were pine trees peeled back and were some 72 feet in length. I was in the eighth grade at the time.[36] I also remember my folks talking about how the

"Fritz" caught fire at Cedar Landing. They said some men chopped it loose from the bank and it drifted out into the river and sank. A man was said to have perished aboard it when it sank just below the Miller place. I think Dan Ward was the Captain at the time it sank.

Ferries were operated by boatmen who used clubs about two-feet long. There were notches cut in the end of the clubs. Steel cables were stretched across the river. The boatmen would pull on the cable with the notched end of the club, thus pulling the barges literally by hand across the river.

Later on I helped with some beekeeping, but this was years ago. I was in partnership with a man in the cattle business, and we were set up along the river between Bruce and Cowford. We used the bees to help pollinate the type grass we had planted for the cattle. Kenna Pate of Bruce still has some bees; he has had them for years. We made mostly Tupelo Honey.[37]

I would like to see the Choctawhatchee River kept with a minimum amount of development. We need to keep the river clean and accessible to the general public. The Northwest Florida Water Management District purchasing it for preservation is the best thing that ever happened. I hope that it can be managed wisely.[38]

32 The Ebro/Bruce Landing along the Choctawhatchee River is actually the "Cowford Public Boat Ramp" and the site of a former community and river ferry. A cattle drive would bring herds from the northern reaches of the county to a place referred to as "High Lonesome," located along the Rock Hill ridge north of Freeport. After overnighting there, the cattle would be pressed on to Cowford where they could be loaded on boats.

33 Habitat and wildlife experts say that no panthers live in the Florida Panhandle, and haven't for decades (less than 200 of the species survive today). However, there are big cats in the Florida Panhandle (of some sort), and there are manifold accounts provided by those who spend time in the outdoors. According to Bruce Hagedorn, a wildlife biologist at Eglin Air Force Base, it is possible that a smaller cat native to Central America, the *jaguarondi*, is present in the area. Regardless, Florida Fish and Wildlife officers get regular calls from residents of the Panhandle about large felines. Those who have seen such animals are hardly convinced of what experts report.

34 The PWA was the Public Works Administration, a governmental economic response to the Great Depression. The PWA, from 1935 to 1944, built a large portion of this nation's infrastructure, including roads, bridges, dams, and housing. In the Florida Panhandle the PWA oversaw the building of the Apalachicola River Bridge, the Panama City Post Office, the Florida Caverns Golf Course, the Pensacola International Airport, the Apalachicola Bay Bridge, the Marianna Municipal Airport, the DeFuniak Springs Post Office, and the US Courthouse in Pensacola.

35 In 1909, the peak of the southern timber industry, more than 16 billion board feet of lumber was produced. By 1932, Florida's annual production of lumber dropped to 320 million board feet. By the 1940s, timber was virtually depleted. For perspective, a thousand square foot structure of the period might take 8,000 board feet of lumber. 1909's production alone would have built two million homes.

36 The first "Destin Bridge" was completed in 1936.

37 See Chapter Eight, "Tupelo," for more information about Tupelo Honey and Kenna Pate.

38 Fisher, *Historical Remembrances*, 35-40.

DOWN BY THE RIVERSIDE

THE SAWMILL LIFE

By Marie Wesley Swinford

Marie "Mickey" Wesley Swinford was born in India, Mississippi, in 1910, and was brought to her home in Point Washington, Florida, at the mouth of the Choctawhatchee River when she was three months old. After graduating from high school in DeFuniak Springs, she studied nursing at Charity Hospital in New Orleans,

Louisiana, receiving her RN degree. Later she enrolled at Florida State College for Women in Tallahassee, and received her BS in Nursing in 1936. She went on to a career in medicine and public health, marrying Dr. Kenneth R. Swinford, a Forestry Professor from the University of Florida.[39]

✳✳✳

My father moved to Point Washington from Ebro. He had several portable sawmills and a permanent mill at Point Washington. He started in the sawmill business with my mother's father, who was a Strickland. The company was known as "Strickland and Wesley" at first. Later it became "Wesley and Sons."[40]

My mother, Katie Marie Strickland Wesley, was visiting my father at one of his portable sawmills in India, Mississippi when I was born. They returned to Point Washington when I was three months old. I imagine we came from Pensacola on the "Fritz" or another boat of similar nature. Steamboats operated on the river back in the day, and I can remember my parents taking them to Pensacola around Christmas to buy presents.

There weren't any good roads, and if you wanted to go anywhere, you traveled mainly by boat. Our trips to DeFuniak Springs required going across the bay in our launch - the "Hazel

S" - and then by car from Freeport. My older brother, Willie, eventually started up a daily ferry service, powered by his boat, the "Lark." He carried the mail to and from Freeport, and a small load of cars. I can remember that sometimes they had moonlight dances on the ferry. I'll never forget these, as my father wouldn't let me participate because I was just a teenager and in his opinion, too young to take part. The State road department later took over the ferry services.[41]

My father had rights to the sunken logs in the Choctawhatchee River. These were from earlier logging and rafting operations. He had his men raise the logs and raft them downstream to his mill at Point Washington. Lumber was sawed at the mill, stored, and partially seasoned on pilings in the entrance to the Point Washington Bayou. Then it was shipped to Pensacola on barges. The remnants of the old pilings are still visible today. Very little evidence is left of the mill, however, except for a few broken bricks that were part of the boiler.[42]

My father also owned quite a bit of land. This included a homestead of 160 acres surrounding and including Eastern Lake that is east of Seagrove Beach. He built a small cottage there and we visited it frequently, either walking or using a horse and buggy. Fishing was great in the lake and we also crabbed, floundered, and collected turtle eggs in the Spring. Eastern Lake was a beautiful, natural place and my father envisioned it becoming a resort area. Unfortunately, the family sold the property after my parents died, several years before the coastal highway was built. We had no idea the property would eventually develop as it has. I think my father and mother would be very unhappy with the way it is today with cottages and condominiums built right on the dunes. My husband and I dislike it so much that we avoid going there anymore.

I used to ride across the bay in the ferry and I went up the river many times on fishing trips. My mother was a great fisherman. She would scull across the bay to her favorite fishing holes along the river or the small creeks emptying into the bay; and later she used a small outboard motor that the boys bought for her. She usually went by herself or took one of the boys with her. I did get to go with her some. I remember the last time I went with her, before I went off the school. We caught about 30 trout.

I went to school at Point Washington through the eighth grade. After that I studied at DeFuniak Springs. My mother was a staunch believer in our getting the best possible education, and she insisted that we go to high school in DeFuniak. She rented a house for me and three of my brothers in DeFuniak and we set up light housekeeping. She would visit on the weekends and help us keep things going. I did most of the cooking for the group, and my brothers helped with the chores. Later I went to nursing school at Charity Hospital in New Orleans. After graduating I got an assistantship in the infirmary at Florida State College for Women. I graduated with my B.S. in nursing in 1936 (Although a graduate of the forerunner of FSU, I'm a Gator supporter now).[43]

My father's sawmill business was burned out three times by people who had grievances against him. I remember the last burning like it was yesterday. I was a little over ten at the time and my father was away at one of his other operations. My mother had heard rumors that some person was out to get the mill. We were ready one night when they set the fire and got it put out quickly. The next night, however, they were able to get a fire going so quickly that we couldn't stop it. The mill burned completely to the ground. My father tried to get enough capital to rebuild, but couldn't pull it off and finally gave it up.

Most of the social life in Point Washington centered around the Methodist Church which my Grandfather Wesley, a Methodist minister, had established.[44] We frequently had dinner on the grounds there with with a lot of singing afterwards. Quite often people would come to our house after services for a hymn-singing session. My mother, who also played the piano for the church, would play and we would all sing along. Away from the church, we used to have picnics at Eastern Lake and sometimes there were dances at Grayton Beach.

Point Washington was a very small community. There were two grocery stores and a post office. During the sawmill era, my father also operated a commissary for his laborers. Most of the people living in Point Washington fished, farmed, and worked at the mill.

39 Fisher, *Historical Remembrances*, 51.

40 Ms. Swinford's father was William Henry Wesley. He built a masterpiece of a home in Point Washington in 1897, the home Swinford grew up in, and where her mother lived until her death in 1953. The house with 10.5 acres was sold, and ten years later sold again to Lois Maxon. Maxon planted and developed gardens on the grounds, and in 1968, she donated the home to the State of Florida, where today "The Wesley House" is the crowning jewel of Eden Gardens State Park.

41 The *Lark* was built of timber from the steamer *Charles E. Cessna*, which carried passengers from the north to Santa Rosa Plantation, otherwise known as Hogtown Bayou. It cost a dollar to make the trip and took over an hour. A free ferry was put in by the state and made several trips per day on schedule. A draw bridge replaced the ferry in 1941.

42 At its peak, Point Washington had several hundred citizens, a school, post office, several stores, and multiple turpentine stills and sawmills.

43 The Florida State College for Women became a coed campus and institution on May 15, 1947.

44 Records indicate that the original Point Washington United Methodist Church was established in 1888 by Swinford's grandfather the Rev. John Wesley, after the congregation met for almost a year at a school. A building was not built until 1893, however, and before that time, it was a traditional brush arbor meeting place. General William Miller and his wife Maria, who named Grayton Beach, donated the land, and the Wesley family donated the lumber.

DOWN BY THE RIVERSIDE

1929

By Ronnie McBrayer

In the spring of 1865, just days after the assassination of President Abraham Lincoln, the Choctawhatchee River experienced the worst flooding in its history. The "Lincoln Flood," as it would become known, washed the city of Geneva, Alabama, and many of its downstream villages, completely away. The residents of Geneva rebuilt their town on higher ground, thinking the Choctawhatchee would never reach them again. They were wrong.

In the spring of 1929, just after Herbert Hoover was sworn in as President, three feet of rain fell on southeast Alabama and Northwest Florida. The Choctawhatchee River, in what became known as the "Hoover Flood," reached a peak of nearly 50 feet at Geneva and almost 30 feet at Ebro, flood levels unmatched to this very day; and the Choctawhatchee Bay rose more than five feet until Destin residents dug a "blowout" channel, largely resulting in the East Pass as we know it today.

Horace Sellers, a young man at the time who worked for the L & N Railroad said, "About four o'clock in the morning somebody knocked on the door and said to get up, that we'd have to go to sandbagging, as the river was rising just like a tide. The railroad grade had washed out, and we were trying to save it. But the water was just like the Bay; we'd fill up a sandbag and throw it in the washout, and the current would take it away like it was a feather. We worked day and night for a week until the water began to go down. It took more than two weeks for railroad traffic to start again. The water was six feet deep in my own house."[45]

In the Choctawhatchee River Basin that includes Holmes, Washington, and Walton Counties, the Hoover Flood of 1929 stranded hundreds of residents on their rooftops for days; logging crews were forced live in the

tree tops until the water receded; 300 homes
and farm buildings were destroyed; more than
2,000 buildings suffered major damage; 3,000
families were displaced or left homeless; and
scores of people died.[46] When the US stock
market collapsed several months later, and the
Great Depression began, it marked for many
Walton County families their toughest days.
This is a part of their collective story.

1929[47]

I

I was born in the summer,
    the year my grandpa died.
And though I never saw his face;
    they say I have his eyes.
He loved the land his father left him;
    and held it in his grip.
All those years of constant sorrow;
    and Yankee shrapnel in his hip.
Like my grandpa, and my father,
      and all my blood from yesteryear;
If I'd had my way, I'd have stayed;
    my home woulda been right there.

II

But in the spring of twenty-nine,
    while living on the Choctaw;
With my father and my mother,

my little sisters and grandma;
It began to rain, felt like forty days,
    with the river on the rise.
Higher than it had ever been,
    since eighteen sixty-five.
Me and father fought that water,
    our trying not enough.
While ma and granny prayed for mercy,
    from the Lord above.

III

The water came up, through the floors;
    Over the windows and over the doors.
Daddy moved us, up to the roof;
    While the lightning and thunder grew.
But Daddy slipped, and then he fell;
    Into the boiling brown swirling hell.
We saw him struggle, in the spray;
        As the current, pulled him away.

IV

I never saw Pa again though I looked for him;
    from Ebro to the Bay.
Along the mud-soaked ground, his body never found;
    he's unburied still today.
Ma weren't no quitter with hand dealt her;
    until the New York market crashed.
And with no money, and being a widow,
    she couldn't pay the courthouse tax.
So come the winter, me and my sisters;
    were took by mama to town.

We left grandma alongside grandpa;
    buried in that muddy ground.

V

It wasn't long, I struck out alone;
    to find work or toil for hire.
Town to town, making boxcar rounds;
    bread lines and train yard fires.
I never again saw my grandpa's land,
    where my father lost his life.
But late at night when the wind is right;
    I hear 'em callin' through the pines.
Lonesome echoes, where do they go?
    haunting, restless mournful cries
Not just for me, but for their land;
    lost in the flood of twenty-nine.

45 Fisher, *Historical Remembrances*, 29.

46 These statistics come from the Geneva, Alabama Public Library System.

47 Words and music of "1929," were created by Ronnie McBrayer specifically for the 2016 stage production of Grit & Grace.

DOWN BY THE RIVERSIDE

SHE DOESN'T NEED A THING

By William A. White

William Avee "W.A." White was born in Point Washington on June 4, 1918, the son of Jesse J. and Dorothy White. He spent his entire life hunting, fishing, and cutting timber on or near the Choctawhatchee River. He married Grace White and they had four children: Gracie Lee, William, Michael Ray, and James William.[48]

Point Washington was like an island at one time. There was no way to get on or off of it except by boat. In the 1930s, I reckon, they started a ferry that ran from Point Washington at the end of the road, to Jolly Bay and then we went by wagon to DeFuniak.

The Wesley boys ran the ferry, and after they ran it for several years, the State put a fee to cross the river: $1.50 to $2.50, I can't remember. Then the State put in a free ferry that ran for years, until they built the bridge around 1940. I walked from Point Washington to Destin in 1930, and there wasn't even a bridge to Fort Walton. You rode a boat. The same for Panama City. All of this was just an island.

The first boat I remember running to Point Washington was a big schooner. George Houseman had the schooner and he hauled freight up the river and to Pensacola.[49] That's the way we got our food. I can remember riding on that boat when we moved here when I was about five years old. They put our old milk cow on it, and she fell overboard. She swam out, got back on the boat, and we carried her on with us. This was about 1923.

That was before the steamboats even started. The "Magnolia" was a sailing schooner and freight boat. But then, when she got too old, they put a steamboat on by the name of the "Fritz." Well, it burned at Cedar Tree up the river. When the river's down real low, you can see a little bit of what didn't burn. It hauled freight. I'd help my daddy cut wood to feed the boat's boiler. We cut a cord of wood for $4.00. We sold about six cords a week to the "Fritz."

Up at the Cowford Landing on the Choctawhatchee River they had an old hand ferry. They had a cable stretched across the river with only hand sticks to pull the thing back and forth with. At the sign that says, "Cowford Fish Camp," is where the ferry used to be. Up on Pine Log Creek, old man Tyler had a ferry.[50] That's how we got off these islands. We had to drive way up there, get on a ferry, and they'd pull you across. It took you the whole day to get to where the ferry was. It would take you two to three days to go anywhere. Old man Miller would ride a horse from here to Vernon. It took him two days.[51]

There was a lot of work to do back then. Not much pay, but a lot of work. And everybody who lived here worked at the same things. There was saw milling, cutting steamboat wood, or cutting cross-ties for the railroad. There wasn't much farming down here. We were the only ones to have a farm. We had seven and a half acres on the river cleared for cultivation. Back during the Depression, we grew what we ate. We'd trade syrup and honey, potatoes, or whatever we had to swap, for clothes to wear from the rolling store that came through. It was a big truck, and you could buy groceries from it. Point Washington was a big business town at one time. There's nothing here now, but there was once three big stores. You could buy everything from a needle to the finest suit of clothes.

Mr. Miller had cattle.[52] Mr. Holly had sheep and cattle. They were the only ones that had any sheep this far south. We had lots of cattle and lots of hogs. The State passed a stock law around 1945, and made us take all our cows and hogs and everything out of these woods.[53] We had to sell or give away our stock – we didn't have any fenced pasture. The St. Joe Paper Company bought all this land up. It only cost him about a dollar an acre, but that much money was hard to get.[54] A teacher only made a dollar a day. A bricklayer got 50 cents a day. You could feed your family on a dollar and a half a week. I worked for three years cutting cross-ties for eight dollars a month, and thought I was doing good.

When it came to fishing, there were a few commercial fishermen in the bay and in the gulf, but snappers were ten cents a pound and grouper sold for two and a half cents a pound. Me and my wife caught mullet and split them all night long for five cents a pound. I used to catch sturgeon as they were going up the river. They come out of the gulf, go up the bay, and come up the river. Me and my wife would catch them with nets, and two or three of them

was all you could put in a pickup truck. They
were eight or nine feet long. The State stopped
us from catching them because they say there
is a shortage of them, but there's nine jillion
of them.

When the flood of 1929 came, the mouth of the
river was just like the Choctawhatchee Bay. It
drowned the cows and everything. It was about
three weeks before we could go home. We were
living in a house that was two feet up off the
ground, and at the time there was only about
two feet above the door that wasn't covered
with water – that was about 20 feet high. We
had a four foot high picket fence back then,
and it was nothing to row a boat right over
the fence and right on into the house. What
will stop floods like that in the future, was
that in 1929, they dug a ditch along the Destin
Pass. It's called East Pass now. The old East
Pass was just a little channel that the river
washed into the gulf.

The river, she doesn't need a thing, except
maybe to stop throwing garbage in it. And
the farmers in Alabama are spraying all the
crops and polluting the bay and killing the
shrimp and everything else in that river.
That's the worst thing that has happened. If
it's wet on the spring, we don't have shrimp
because the farmers spray pesticides, then we
get big rains, and the runoff pollutes the
river. Trucks have to spray for mosquitoes

in the ditches, and lots of crawfish will be lying there dead. They don't realize all they are killing. When I was a young-un, I could drink water right out of that ditch, because there was no spraying going on. I believe it would kill you now.

48 Fisher, *Historical Remembrances*, 63.

49 George Washington Houseman (1869-1936) was a teenager living in Freeport, Florida at the time of the 1885 Census, part of mariner family. Houseman is buried in Point Washington.

50 Just south of Ebro there is Tyler Ferry Road, accessible via Highway 20.

51 Exactly which "old man Miller" this is appears impossible to know, but looking at genealogical records it is almost certainly Mr. William Leslie Miller (1859-1939). Miller, with his wife Mary Roberson (nee Stanley) raised a half-dozen children on Grayton Beach. His grandson, Malcolm Patterson, was Walton County's first Tourist Development Council Director (1988-2000), and he regularly rode horses on South Walton's beaches, saying "We rounded up cattle just like they do in Texas...Let me tell ya what, you could ride from Destin to Inlet Beach and never see anything but cow dung."

52 Ibid.

53 "Open range" ended in Florida in 1949 with passage of the Warren Act.

54 "Him" needed no explanation for Floridians of the time period: Alfred I. Du Pont, though Du Pont died before the largest Florida land purchases were made. Du Pont's successor, his brother-in-law, Edward Gresham Ball, would lead the St. Joe Company in meteoric levels of land acquisition in the Florida Panhandle. W.A. White was correct; for only dollars per acre, St. Joe eventually held more than a million acres of coastal land. Additionally, the company acquired the Apalachicola Railroad and built a paper mill in the city of St. Joe in 1938. The St. Joe paper mill, while profitable, was an environmental and ecological disaster. Mercifully, after six decades, St. Joe got out of the paper business. Today, St. Joe remains one of the largest land owners in Florida, and has successfully pivoted from paper products to real estate development. The communities of Watercolor and Watersound in Walton County are St. Joe properties.

DOWN BY THE RIVERSIDE

THE BRIDGE

By Verna Hughes

Here is another tale from Verna Hughes, the daughter of George B. Hughes and Hortie Mella Gillman. See the introduction to "Chapter Three: At The Yancey House," for further biographical information.

I recall a time when Mrs. Lillie Motley, Mr.
Henry's wife, was on her way to see her brother
who lived south of us, across the creek. She
was on a Jersey Wagon which was hitched to
old Pet, their mule.

In those days, road and bridge maintenance
was not the greatest, and sometimes they were
in bad need of repair.[55] The bridge across the
creek was made of two-by-eight oak boards
nailed crosswise on sleepers, with runways
then nailed down lengthwise for the wheels
of cars and wagons to run on. Pet had crossed
the bridge many times, but on two or three
occasions the boards were lose, and some were
missing. One time Pet actually fell through a
large hole where the boards were missing, and
had to be pried and lifted out, as she was not
able to get out herself.

On this particular day, Mrs. Lillie was
halfway across the bridge as old Pet, walking
slowly and cautiously along, came to a gaping
hole in the middle of the bridge. Seeing the
hole, she stopped. Mrs. Lillie began to urge
her on, but Pet wouldn't budge. In fact, as Mrs.
Lillie continued to slap the reins and yell,
Pet began to back up. Mrs. Lillie was shouting,
"Whoa, Pet whoa!" and was pulling back on
the reins. Pet kept backing up, and the wagon
began to turn crossways of the bridge.

The seat on which she was sitting was one
that set on the edge of the wagon body in

slots. As the back wheels of the wagon went off the side of the bridge, the wagon seat began to slide backward down the wagon body, with Mrs. Lille praying loudly and hanging on for dear life. As the back end of the wagon dropped off the bridge – some four or five feet – and the seat hit the back end of the wagon, Mrs. Lillie landed bottom up in a bunch of low bushes. She wasn't hurt, but was sorely frightened. She got up, shouting praises and thanking God for protection.

The mule, standing quite still all the while, was taken loose from the wagon and led off the bridge. The wagon was finally gotten back onto the bridge. Mrs. Lillie called off her trip to her brother's house until a later time.

There was another occurrence that happened at the same bridge. However, it had to do with my sister Lois walking home with Ida Pearl and Isabel Scott, who lived across the creek. After they left, my brother Rubert and Carl Motley decided to scare them as they came back home later.

Rubert had a device that was called a dumb-bull. This item was made of a piece of cowhide stretched tightly across one end of a piece of hollow log with thin sides. In the middle of the cowhide there was a small hole, through which a rawhide string had been thrust. This string was well coated with resin and, when wrapped with a small piece of cowhide and pulled smartly, a very loud, hideous booming, roaring sound could be fetched from it.

The boys decided to get under the bridge with that dumb-bull. While Rubert worked it, Carl planned to climb up on the side of the bridge under a sheet. They were sure the girls would scream and run in terror. Daddy told them to be sure to let the girls get on the end of the bridge toward the house before they did anything, so the girls wouldn't run or jump off the bridge and hurt themselves.

The boys positioned themselves under the bridge about middle way and waited for the girls. There was a fair moon, and one could see quite well. Finally, the girls came walking across the bridge, laughing and talking, and chewing some sugar cane. The boys let them get just past them and Rubert pulled the dumb-bull, making a hideous noise. The laughing and talking from the girls stopped. Rubert did it again, and one of the girls screamed. Carl began to climb up on the side of the bridge under the sheet, and the Scott girl really did become scared.

Lois called out, "All right, Rubert! You better get back, or I'll hit you with this stalk of cane!"

As she advanced toward the form under the sheet, Carl called out, "Don't hit me, Lois! It's Carl!"

He pulled off the sheet and one of the

girls told him how mean he was to try to scare them like that. They all walked up the hill together to the house. No one got to see them run up the hill as planned.

---

55 "In those days," was the period of years near the Great Depression.

DOWN BY THE RIVERSIDE

CYPRESS AND SNAG-BOATS

By James Lamar Ward

This final excerpt from the "Historical Remembrances" booklet is a treasure, as James Lamar Ward is exceptional with his historical details and narrative, as well he should be.[56] Mr. Ward was one of the more accomplished men Walton County produced in the 20th Century. A lifelong resident of the Freeport community with his wife Wanda Burl, nee Johnson, he was a teacher (for 35 years), school board member, mayor, business owner, and in his youth, a snag-boat hand on the Choctawhatchee River. J. Lamar Ward died August 4, 1991, and is buried alongside his wife at Hatcher Cemetery.

***

The McCaskills owned a big mill right down where the bayou goes into the bay, at a place called Beatrice Point. It had big band saws. The mill burned somewhere around 1913. I remember the day it burned, I remember exactly what my brother and I were doing, but I don't remember the exact date.[57]

There've been three pullings of cypress around here. They used a pull-boat to get the cypress logs out of the swamp. The first pull-boat was a big one. It had a big steel cable. It must have been an inch-and-a-half or two-inch cable. The two pull-boats my daddy ran were made of four to six inch "deals." A deal is a square timber. The pull-boats were massively built; they had to be. The machinery was bolted down on the deck. The first one had two big wenches and a set of "donkey" engines – steam powered engines.

To get the cypress logs out of the swamp, the workmen would cut a trail in to where the logs were. They took a steel cable and dragged it to the logs. With the cable they took a huge steel block. The block was chained to a big tree. The cable was then looped through the block and dragged back to the pull-boat. It was a huge job because the trees were huge. They would drag logs several hundred yards through the swamp. Some of them are still down there. If you go up the East River fork and go out on the island, you'll find some. Last time I was there, I found some my granddaddy had cut. Cypress was cut with axes – a massive job. In high water, believe it or not, they'd cut a notch in the tree and stick a board in so they could perch up there and still cut trees when the water was high.

During World War I we all got the Spanish Flu. My brother Jack brought it back from Pensacola. He was firing a boiler down there at Ft. Pickens, and got it there. The flu killed people going and coming, so we tried to stay isolated. I'd come and get the mail in a skiff boat with instructions not to stop anywhere between the landing and the post office. Mama told me, "Don't go there and wait. If there is a big crowd, just hold back. Then get the mail and leave." But all of us got it. The epidemic lasted about a year. It started slowly but spread rapidly after. It killed many. It was tragic.[58]

The last mill was the Geneva Mill and it blew its last whistle on January 15, 1931. They scrapped our sawmill and sent it to Mobile for junk. The Japanese bought every bit they could get — so they could shoot it back at us. That's really what happened. My brother was in the Merchant Marines. He bought a set of books that gave a picture and the name of the navy of every country. He told me, "You just wait. People don't realize what Japan has — they have a powerful navy." He knew what they had. Our government knew it too.[59]

Anyhow, the steamboats docked down on Fourmile Creek below Freeport in front of the warehouses. There was a wharf down there where that bridge on Fourmile Creek is now. Except for one little space there, there were warehouses for a hundred yards, warehouse after warehouse. There was a cooper shop down there also, and a big turpentine still up on the hill. The cooper shop made barrels for the still and the turpentine went to Pensacola on steamboats.

One fellow floated out of the sinking of the "Belle" on a big feather pillow with a canvas cover. But other people drowned when the "Belle" went down.[60] The "Vernon" burned and sank at Rooks Bluff. The "Eugene" in its old days was parked at Wise Bluff and the caretaker let it sink. The old "Fritz" was up here at Cedar Tree Landing and it caught fire and drifted down river. As a steamboat burns and loses its load, it rises and keeps on burning except for the very bottom. I don't know if they recovered anything off the "Fritz," but Nathan McGiver, an old man who lived out here in the woods, went to the "Eugene" and got the boiler. He disconnected it, pumped the water out of it, and with strapped cross-ties and a paddle, floated it down the river. It went to Point Washington over yonder and the Wesleys pulled it out on the hill and used it to run a sawmill. That was along in the 1920s, I imagine.

We got out groceries and gasoline off a steamboat; they came wholesale from Pensacola. If we hadn't placed an order, they'd open up somebody else's groceries and sell us some. Poppa paid the $2.00 deposit on a Standard Oil drum. The gasoline hardly cost that much. My brother and I, when we'd hear the steamboat blow, we were ready. We took one of our skiff boats and went out there with the empty drum. Jack would pull as hard as he could, and I'd stand in the bow and throw them a rope. They'd hold us by the rope, take our drum out, fill it with gasoline, and put the drum back in the bottom of the boat. Then they slowed the steamboat down to give us a chance to push off. If the skiff ever got under the paddlewheel, well, that'd be the end of you.

The steamboats would charge a three dollar fare for travel, and that included your meals. It took all day to get to Pensacola. You left Freeport in the morning and stopped at the mouth of Alaqua Bayou, where the Gulf Red Cypress Company had a big mill.[61] It went on up to the landing at Portland. It went in at Rocky Bayou, at Niceville, and at Mary Ester. There was a stop, a stop, a stop, and it didn't go very fast anyway.

I got married in 1924 and went to work on the snag-boat, "Choctawhatchee" for $50 a month and board. The snag-boat worked all the way up to Geneva. It was a butt-headed vessel with a paddlewheel. It had big, triple blocks, a snatch-block pulley, and a steel winch. I worked as the turn holder.[62]

56 Fisher, *Historical Remembrances*, 57-62.

57 Robert E. Lee McCaskill was born June 4, 1871, of old Scottish stock, in the Eucheeanna Valley of Walton County. He assumed apprenticeship in his father's timber and land business - the J.J. (John Jett) McCaskill Company, before establishing the R.E.L. McCaskill Company, relocating to DeFuniak Springs after the sawmill fire of 1912. The "McCaskill House," a large, beautiful old home on Four Mile Creek just a few miles from Beatrice Point, still stands. As of this writing it is being restored by local resident Kevin Bloom.

58 The Spanish Flu of 1918 infected more than a quarter of the US population and killed almost 700,000 Americans. More than 40,000 of these deaths were servicemen mobilized during the last days of World War I.

59 Mr. Ward's observation is astute. Much of the raw material, especially metal, that Japan used to build its military might came from the United States. These materials were traded under the 1911 *Treaty of Commerce and Navigation between the United States and Japan*. Washington did not cease the terms of this treaty until 1939.

60 "While enroute to Pensacola yesterday afternoon the river steamer 'Belle,' of Vernon, Fla., encountered severe winds in the Choctawhatchee river, sank to the bottom and four lives were lost: The captain, engineer, and two children who were passengers. The 'Belle' was loaded with naval stores and it is suggested that the load was too heavy for safe navigation in the fifty-mile gale. The dead: Ed Burlison, of Pensacola Captain; Charley Belle, of Vernon, engineer; two children, names not learned. The cargo valued at five thousand dollars will probably prove a total loss. The sad incident was reported on the arrival of the Swan from Boggy Bayou this afternoon at three o'clock. The Swan brought the body of the dead captain, who was a well known citizen of Pensacola" (From *The Pensacola Evening News*, April 27, 1911).

61 The Gulf Red Cypress Company was based in Savannah, Georgia. The company incorporated in Florida in 1935, but had dissolved five years later.

62 The "Choctawhatchee" appears in multiple annual reports of the US Army Corps of Engineers throughout the 1920s. Along with the "Choctawhatchee," three other snag boats are mentioned: The *Escambia, Geneva, and Conecuh,* all working the Gulf coast and operated by hired labor.

DOWN BY THE RIVERSIDE

ROLL ON CHOCTAWHATCHEE

By Ronnie McBrayer

This original song might be an appropriate conclusion to this little book. So long as the Choctawhatchee "rolls on," it will provide perennial enjoyment for generations of Walton County and Panhandle residents. May we, and those who follow us, be good stewards of this beautiful river and the lands that surround it.

Roll On Choctawhatchee[63]

Up in the morning, before the dawn;
    chasing this river to its end.
Here's hoping today, the wind and the wave;
    will somehow be my friend.
Alone in the dark, with only the stars;
    and that big old moon to light my way.
Before this days ends, I'll be home again;
    with the sun's setting rays.

Roll on, Choctawhatchee;
Lead me down to the sea.
Wash away all my troubles;
Leave my soul fresh and clean.
Let your rolling waters;
Take me to the coming dawn.
May the morning breeze, set me free;
As the Choctawhatchee rolls on.

This sanctuary, God made for me;
    is built from the air and the water.
This boat is my pew, under skies of blue;
    and this river is my altar.
It's here that I pray, at breaking of day;

as the morning whippoorwills rejoice.
And the cypress trees, on the bayou beach;
join in with one voice.

Roll on, Choctawhatchee;
Lead me down to the sea.
Wash away all my troubles;
Leave my soul fresh and clean.
Let your rolling waters;
Take me to the coming dawn.
May the morning breeze, set me free;
As the Choctawhatchee rolls on.

Heaven's blowing in the morning breeze;
As angels mingle with the honey bees.
On this river is where I come alive;
Born again and baptized.

63 An original song with words and music by Ronnie McBrayer, 2016.

ABOUT THE AUTHOR

Scientists say that the beautiful, sugar-white beaches of the Florida Panhandle are the result of erosion from the Appalachian Mountains. A sand dune that we enjoy today, as we are told, was once a mountain top in Georgia, but over time that mountain washed all the way down to the sea. There's no better description for writer, Ronnie McBrayer.

Before making his home near the beautiful beaches of Walton County, Florida more than a decade ago, Ronnie was a life-long Georgian, born and raised in the foothills of the Appalachian Mountains. Today, having washed down to the sea, he is the author of multiple books and publications, a talented musician, a local pastor, and a nationally syndicated columnist.

Ronnie maintains a contagious faith, a cheerful schoolboy wit, and an applauded storytelling style that invites his readers and listeners to discover new ways to experience personal freedom and grace. With his wife Cindy – a talented artist in her own right – and his three sons, Ronnie might be a long way from home, but he is never far from his roots. Visit his website at www.ronniemcbrayer.net.

Made in the USA
Charleston, SC
07 March 2017